NCERT Practice

WorkBook

English
Marigold

CLASS
01

Emmanuel D'Souza
Gloria D'Souza

arihant

Arihant Prakashan (School Division Series)

arihant

Arihant Prakashan (School Division Series)

Administrative & Production Offices

Regd. Office
'Ramchhaya' 4577/15, Agarwal Road, Darya Ganj, New Delhi -110002
Tele: 011- 47630600, 43518550

Head Office
Kalindi, TP Nagar, Meerut (UP) - 250002
Tel: 0121-7156203, 7156204

Sales & Support Offices
Agra, Ahmedabad, Bengaluru, Bareilly, Chennai, Delhi, Guwahati, Hyderabad, Jaipur, Jhansi, Kolkata, Lucknow, Nagpur & Pune.

PO No : TXT-XX-XXXXXXX-X-XX

Published by Arihant Publications (India) Ltd.

For further information about the books published by Arihant, log on to www.arihantbooks.com or e-mail at info@arihantbooks.com

Follow us on  

PRODUCTION TEAM

Publishing Managers
Keshav Mohan, Amit Verma

Project Coordinator
Manju

Project Editor
Amit Tanwar

Cover Designer
Bilal Hashmi

Inner Designer
Ankit Saini

Proof Readers
Akash Agarwal

Workbook, Why?

"Knowledge will not be with you for Long Unless You Practice"

This quotation answer the above question 'Workbook, Why ?'
perfectly, i.e Workbooks are made to give the students practice required to achieve
perfection and mastery in the subject. These are the only Workbooks, which are strictly
based on NCERT, the only recommended books by Govt. of India & CBSE (reference
Circular No. Acad-41/2015 dated 20th July 2015).

Given below is the detailed description of Workbook and some of its special features

ONLY COMPLETE WORKBOOK BASED ON NCERT

NCERT textbooks are the only textbooks, which have been prepared according to
National Curriculum Framework, which discourages the idea of rote learning rather
focus on inculcating creativity & initiative in the students to make them participants in
learning not just a receiver of a one-way communication.

Keeping the importance of NCERT textbooks in mind we have prepared this Workbook,
strictly based on NCERT content, this Workbook will complement NCERT by providing
practice on the material given in each chapter of NCERT textbook. This is the only
Workbook, which covers complete Syllabus of English.

WORKBOOK- PURPOSE, USE & FEATURES

This Workbook, through its numerous exercises having different variety of questions
covering practical importance of English & Day-to-Day communication, will prove to be
equally useful for both, Classroom and at Home. One more purpose of this Workbook
is to provide the students a systematic practice of the content taught in the class and
what they study in the textbooks.

Some special features of this workbook are

- Complete coverage of two Sections; Literature and Grammar

- Complete coverage of all the Chapters of the NCERT Textbook

- Different variety of questions; Fill in the Blanks, True-False, Matching, Multiple
  Choice Questions, Very Short Answer, Short Answer Type etc.

WORKBOOK-DESIGNED TO IMPROVE SUBJECT ABILITIES

All the material given in this workbook is tailored to suit subject content with equal
support on learning, which will surely help students to boost their abilities and
confidence in the subject.

I look forward for the feedback from students, teachers and parents for the further
improvement of the contents of this book. I will try to update the contents according to
your feedback in further editions of this Workbook.

The Publisher

Contents

01

A Happy Child

Text Based Questions

1. State 'T' for True and 'F' for False statement.

(i) The house of the child is red.

(ii) The child in the poem is a sad child.

(iii) The colour of the tree is yellow.

(iv) There are two trees in the child's house.

(v) The child sits under the tree.

2. Tick (✓) the correct option.

(i) The child's house is ___________ .

(a) big   (b) clean

(c) dirty   (d) little

(ii) What does the child do the whole day?

(a) Cry   (b) Sing

(c) Laugh and play   (d) Draw

(iii) The colour of the tree is ___________ .

    (a) white   ☐   (b) green   ☐

    (c) black   ☐   (d) blue   ☐

(iv) The child hardly ever ___________ .

    (a) cries   ☐   (b) laughs   ☐

    (c) sleeps   ☐   (d) speaks   ☐

3. On the basis of the poem, give answers to the following questions.

    (i) What does the child do under the tree after playing? (Sits/Sleeps)

    (ii) Which tree does the child have? (Green/Yellow)

Language Based Questions

4. Circle the words which are correctly spelled.

	A	B	C
(i)	Undar	Under	Underr
(ii)	Laugh	Logh	Loagh
(iii)	Whol	Wholl	Whole
(iv)	Shade	Shaade	Shadee
(v)	Hoase	House	Houss
(vi)	Oftan	Oftenn	Often

5. Write the names of the following pictures.

(i)　　　　　(ii)　　　　　(iii)

_______________　　_______________　　_______________

6. Complete the missing letters to form words from the poem.

(i) R __ D   (ii) P __ A __

(iii) D __ Y   (iv) L __ U __ H

(v) G __ E __ N   (vi) S __ N

7. Identify the parts of the house and write their names in the box. Also, colour the house.

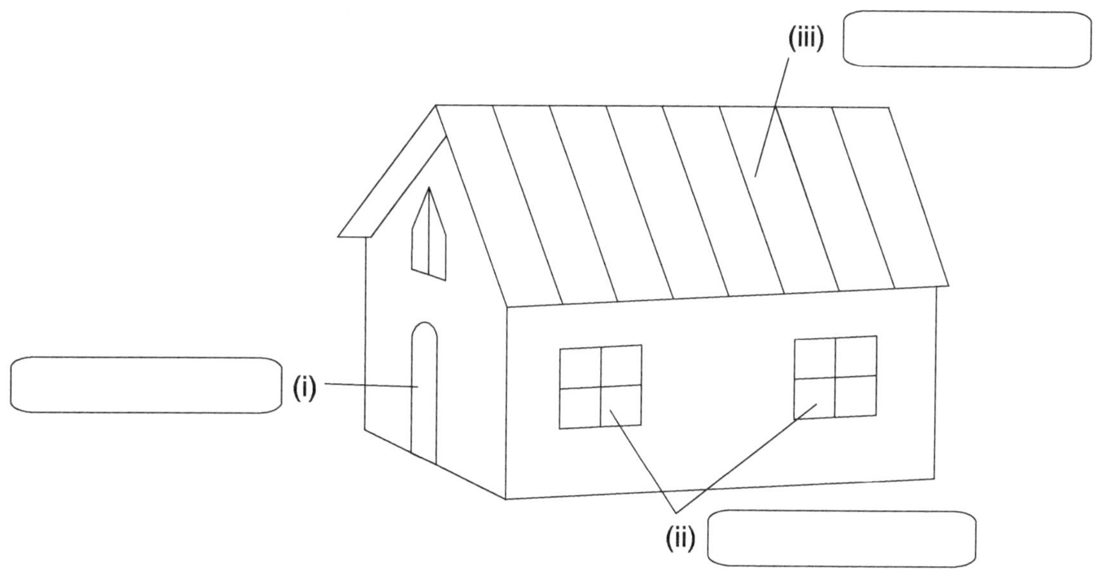

02

Three Little Pigs

Text Based Questions

1. State 'T' for True and 'F' for False statement.

   (i) There are four pigs in the story.

   (ii) Sonu lived in a house of straw.

   (iii) The names of the pigs were Sonu, Monu and Nonu.

   (iv) The wolf blew away Monu's house.

   (v) The brick house was green in colour.

2. Tick (✓) the correct option.

   (i) Gonu lived in a house of __________ .

     (a) straw   (b) sticks

     (c) mud   (d) bricks

(ii) The wolf was ________ .

    (a) good   (b) small

    (c) big and bad   (d) very good

(iii) The wolf huffed and ________ .

    (a) stuffed   (b) puffed

    (c) huffed   (d) laughed

(iv) The brick house was ________ .

    (a) very strong   (c) weak

    (c) very weak   (d) strong

3. On the basis of the chapter, give answers to the following questions.

    (i) What kind of house did Monu live in? (Sticks/Bricks)

    (ii) Who came to Sonu's house one day? (Monu/Wolf)

    (iii) Who ran to Gonu's house? (Wolf/Sonu and Monu)

    (iv) Who all lived happily together in the red brick house?
        (Wolf and Little Pigs/Sonu, Monu and Gonu)

    (v) What was the colour of the brick house in which they lived happily
        together? (Yellow/Red)

Language Based Questions

4. Match the words in Column A with their opposites in Column B.

Column A	Column B
(i) Big	(a) Weak
(ii) Bad	(b) Go
(iii) Down	(c) Good
(iv) Strong	(d) Small
(v) Come	(e) Up

5. Circle the words which are spelled correctly.

	A	B	C
(i)	Strau	Straw	Stroy
(ii)	Sticks	Stecks	Stycks
(iii)	Happyly	Happily	Hapyly
(iv)	Togather	Twogether	Together
(v)	Varyy	Viry	Very
(vi)	Bricks	Brikks	Brikys

01 After a Bath

Text Based Questions

1. State 'T' for True and 'F' for False statement.

(i) The child in the poem wipes before he takes a bath.

(ii) The child has a shiny nose.

(iii) A dog takes more time to dry.

(iv) The child wishes to be a dog.

2. Fill in the blanks from the box given below.

shiny, toes, wipe, two

(i) Hands to _____________

(ii) and fingers and _____________

(iii) and _____________ wet legs

(iv) and a _____________ nose

3. Tick (✓) the correct option.

(i) The boy tries to wipe himself till he is _____________ .

 (a) wet   (b) dry

 (c) sad   (d) happy

(ii) What do you use to dry yourself after a bath?

(a) Soap   ☐   (b) Toothpaste ☐

(c) Cream   ☐   (d) Towel ☐

(iii) A dog takes less time to ___________ .

(a) cry   ☐   (b) fry ☐

(c) dry   ☐   (d) buy ☐

4. On the basis of the poem, give answers to the following questions.

(i) How many legs have been mentioned in the poem? (Three/Two)

____

(ii) Can you bath yourself? (Yes/No)

____

(iii) Which body part is used to wipe in the poem? (Toes/Hands)

____

Language Based Questions

5. Circle the words which are spelled correctly.

	A	B	C
(i)	Tri	Try	Trry
(ii)	Wip	Wipee	Wipe
(iii)	Fingars	Fingirs	Fingers
(iv)	Toes	Toees	Tois
(v)	Coldd	Could	Coud
(vi)	Sheke	Skakke	Shake

6. Write the opposites of the following words.

(i) Dry _______________   (ii) Shiny _______________

(iii) Less _______________   (iv) After _______________

7. Write the things you need to take a bath using the picture clues.

(i) B __ C __ __ T 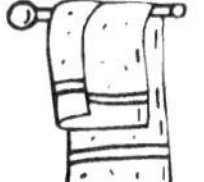   (ii) T __ W __ L

(iii) S __ __ P

8. Label the different parts of your body using the words in the box.

> Head, Mouth, Chest, Fingers, Arm, Foot, Nose, Neck, Tummy, Leg, Hand, Toes

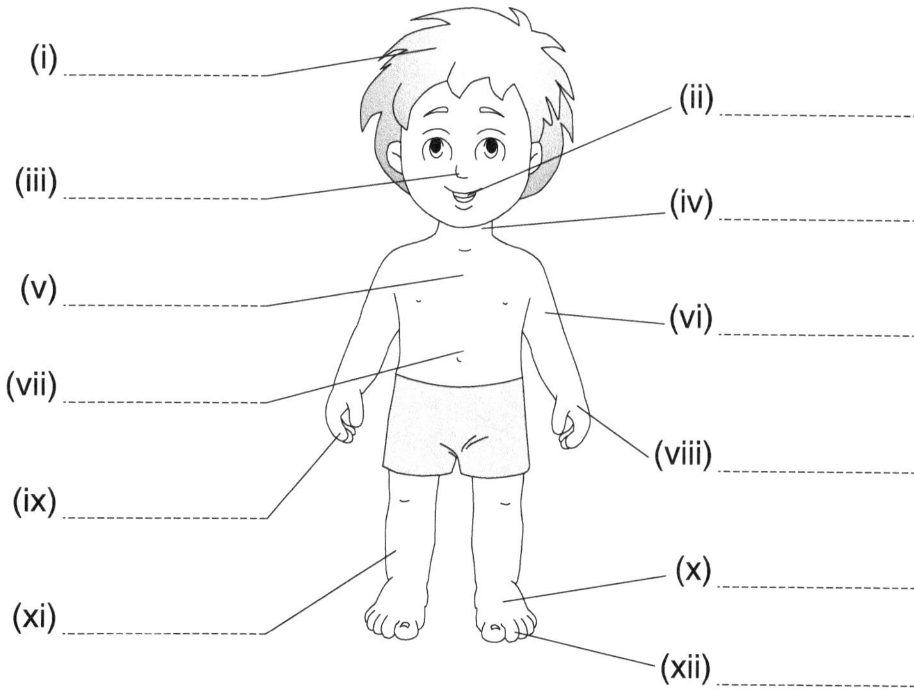

(i) _______________

(ii) _______________

(iii) _______________

(iv) _______________

(v) _______________

(vi) _______________

(vii) _______________

(viii) _______________

(ix) _______________

(x) _______________

(xi) _______________

(xii) _______________

02

The Bubble, the Straw and the Shoe

Text Based Questions

1. State 'T' for True and 'F' for False statement.

(i) Bubble, Straw and Shoe were not friends.

(ii) They knew how to cross the river.

(iii) Straw stretched himself from one bank to the other.

(iv) Straw broke when Shoe jumped on it.

(v) The Bubble started crying when the Shoe fell in the water.

2. Tick (✓) the correct option.

(i) The Shoe wanted to float on __________ .

(a) Straw   (b) Bubble

(c) both Straw and Bubble   (d) River

(ii) Who suggested that straw should stretch himself from one bank to the other?

(a) Straw   (b) Shoe

(c) Bubble   (d) River

(iii) There was a _________ when the Shoe fell into the water.

    (a) big bang   (b) bang

    (c) splash   (d) loud splash

3. On the basis of the chapter, give answers to the following questions.

(i) Where did Bubble, Straw and Shoe go one day? (River/Forest)

____

(ii) Who said Bubble, "Let us float on you?" (Shoe/Straw)

____

(iii) On whom did the Shoe jump? (Straw/Bubble)

____

Language Based Questions

4. Circle the correctly spelled words from the following.

	A	B	C
(i)	Strew	Straww	Straw
(ii)	Forast	Forest	Forrest
(iii)	River	Rivar	Rivarr
(iv)	Croas	Cross	Crose

5. Match the words in Column A with their opposites in Column B.

Column A	Column B
(i) Float	(a) Old
(ii) Live	(b) Sink
(iii) Loud	(c) Die
(iv) Wet	(d) Soft
(v) Young	(e) Dry

6. Complete the following words by filling the missing letters.

(i) T __ ME

(ii) S __ OE

(iii) R __ V __ R

(iv) F __ O __ T

(v) Y __ U

(vi) C _ O _ S

7. Pick out the items from the box which will float on water.

Nail	Glass	Pencil Box	Pencil	Rubber	Sharpner
Straw	Shoes	Ball	Bat	Paper Boat	

The items that would float on water are __________

__________ .

01

One Little Kitten

Text Based Questions

1. State 'T' for True and 'F' for False statement.

  (i) The kitten is big.

  (ii) The seals in the poem are sad.

  (iii) The bees in the poem are not brave.

  (iv) There are twelve fleas in the poem.

  (v) The eels in the poem are also sad.

2. Tick (✓) the correct option.

  (i) There are __________ big cats in the poem.

    (a) four   (b) two

    (c) three   (d) many

(ii) The seagulls are ________ .

    (a) sad   ☐   (b) fat   ☐

    (c) intelligent   ☐   (d) silly   ☐

(iii) The elephants are ________ .

    (a) smelly   ☐   (b) nervous   ☐

    (c) fat   ☐   (d) brave   ☐

(iv) The donkeys have ________ .

    (a) tails   ☐   (b) scales   ☐

    (c) bags   ☐   (d) pencils   ☐

3. On the basis of the poem, give answers to the following questions.

    (i) How many lizards are there in the poem? (Five/Nine)

    (ii) How are the rats? (Small/Big)

    (iii) What type of butterflies are mentioned in the poem? (Baby/Silly)

Language Based Questions

4. Circle the words which are spelled correctly.

	A	**B**	**C**
(i)	Buttarfly	Butterfly	Butterfli
(ii)	Sily	Silli	Silly
(iii)	Nervous	Nervos	Nerwous
(iv)	Brawe	Brave	Bravee
(v)	Alligator	Alligetor	Aligattor

5. Write the plural of the following.

(i) Butterfly _______________   (ii) Kitten _______________

(iii) Fish _______________   (iv) Rat _______________

(v) Seagull _______________

6. Match the words in Column A with their opposites in Column B.

Column A	**Column B**
(i) Fat	(a) Coward
(ii) Sad	(b) Thin
(iii) Brave	(c) Happy
(iv) Nervous	(d) Intelligent
(v) Silly	(e) Calm

7. Complete the words from the poem by filling up the missing letters.

(i) O __ E   (ii) B __ BY

(iii) F __ UR   (iv) S __ D

(v) S __ LLY   (vi) B __ ES

(vii) T __ ILS

02

Lalu and Peelu

Text Based Questions

1. State 'T' for True and 'F' for False statement.

(i) The hen had two chicks.

(ii) Lalu was yellow.

(iii) Peelu loved yellow things.

(iv) The red chilli was very sweet.

(v) Peelu brought a yellow laddu for Lalu.

(vi) Lalu's mouth started burning after eating the laddu.

2. Tick (✓) the correct option.

(i) Lalu loved _______ things.

(a) yellow   (b) red

(c) orange   (d) blue

(ii) The red chilli was on the _______ .

(a) tree   (b) plate

(c) plant   (d) grass

(iii) Who came running when Lalu's mouth was burning?

(a) Lalu's Friend   (b) Lalu's father

(c) Lalu's Uncle   (d) Mother Hen

(iv) Who kissed Peelu?

(a) Lalu

(b) Mother Hen

(c) Both Mother Hen and Lalu

(d) Chilli

3. On the basis of the chapter, give answers to the following questions.

(i) What was the colour of Peelu? (Green/Yellow)

(ii) What did Lalu eat one day? (Red Chilli/Laddu)

(iii) What did Lalu do when his mouth started burning?

(Gobbled/Screamed)

(iv) Lalu loved things of which colour?

Language Based Questions

4. Circle the correctly spelled words in each cloud.

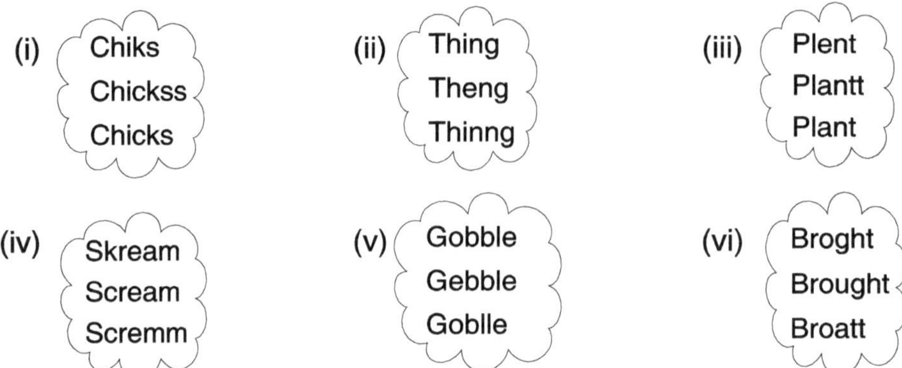

5. Match the words in Column A with their opposites in Column B.

Column A	Column B
(i) Hot	(a) Down
(ii) Stop	(b) Hate
(iii) Love	(c) Start
(iv) Up	(d) Cold

6. Look at the picture and answer the questions. Also, colour the picture.

(i) Who all do you see in the picture?

(ii) What is Peelu carrying in his mouth?

01

Once I Saw a Little Bird

Text Based Questions

1. State 'T' for True and 'F' for False statement.

  (i) The bird was big.

  (ii) The bird was hopping.

  (iii) The child went to the window.

  (iv) The bird shook his head.

  (v) The bird kept sitting.

2. Tick (✓) the correct option.

  (i) The child saw a ___________ .

    (a) elephant   (b) tree

    (c) window   (d) bird

(ii) The child wanted the bird to _________ .

    (a) shop ☐   (b) dance ☐

    (c) stop ☐   (d) eat ☐

(iii) How many birds are there in the poem?

    (a) One ☐   (b) Two ☐

    (c) Three ☐   (d) Four ☐

(iv) The bird flew _________ .

    (a) in ☐   (b) at ☐

    (c) away ☐   (d) inside ☐

3. On the basis of the poem give answers to the following questions.

    (i) What did the child cry? (Little bird/Hop)

____

    (ii) What did the bird do when the child reached the window? (Hop/Shook)

____

Language Based Questions

4. Write the opposites of the following words.

    (i) Little _____________   (ii) Start _____________

    (iii) Go _____________   (iv) Cry _____________

02

Mittu and the Yellow Mango

Text Based Questions

1. State 'T' for True and 'F' for False statement.

(i) Mittu was a red parrot with a green beak.

(ii) Mittu loved to fly.

(iii) Mittu was not afraid of the crow.

(iv) The crow had a very loud voice.

(v) The mango was not nice.

2. Tick (✓) the correct option.

(i) There was a big _______ mango on a tree.

(a) red

(b) green

(c) white

(d) yellow

(ii) The crow was __________ .

   (a) big   (b) black

   (c) big and black   (d) small

(iii) Mittu pecked the balloon with his __________ .

   (a) head   (b) beak

   (c) feathers   (d) tail

(iv) The crow thought that a big ________ was after him.

   (a) gun   (b) man

   (c) woman   (d) hunter

3. On the basis of the chapter, give answers to the following questions.

(i) What did Mittu want to eat? (Mangoes/Oranges)

____

(ii) Where was the mango? (In house/On tree)

____

(iii) What was Mittu afraid of? (Parrot/Crow)

____

(iv) What did Mittu see under the tree? (Balloon/Mango)

Language Based Questions

4. Circle the words which are spelled correctly.

	A	B	C
(i)	Beek	Beak	Beake
(ii)	Black	Bleck	Bllack
(iii)	Afraidd	Afraid	Afradd
(iv)	Balloonn	Ballonn	Balloon
(v)	Pekked	Peckid	Pecked
(vi)	Carefull	Careful	Carefal
(vii)	Noisse	Nois	Noise
(viii)	Clevar	Clevr	Clever

5. Match the words in Column A with their opposites in Column B.

Column A		Column B	
(i)	Down	(a)	Off
(ii)	Clever	(b)	Up
(iii)	Afraid	(c)	Careless
(iv)	Careful	(d)	Unafraid
(v)	On	(e)	Foolish

01

Merry-Go-Round

Text Based Questions

1. State 'T' for True and 'F' for False statement.

(i) The merry-go-round went straight.

(ii) The child climbed on a big brown horse.

(iii) The horse went round and round.

(iv) The child rode around on the merry-go-round.

2. Tick (✓) the correct option.

(i) The child climbed _______ on the merry-go-round.

(a) down   (b) up

(c) at   (d) in

(ii) The horse was _______ in colour.

(a) black   (b) white

(c) brown   (d) grey

3. On the basis of the poem give answers to the following questions.

(i) Where did the child sit? (Horse/Camel)

(ii) How did the merry-go-round go? (Around and round/Round and round)

Language Based Questions

4. Circle the correctly spelled words from the following.

	A	**B**	**C**
(i)	Rondd	Round	Roand
(ii)	Broun	Brownn	Brown
(iii)	Meri	Merry	Mirry
(iv)	Climbed	Climbd	Climbbd
(v)	Arond	Arondd	Around

5. Write the opposites of the following words.

(i) Big

(ii) Run

(iii) On

(iv) White

02

Circle

Text Based Questions

1. State 'T' for True and 'F' for False statement.

   (i) Grandmother drew a circle.

   (ii) Grandmother drew four lines on the circle.

   (iii) Mohini told her grandmother how to make a balloon.

   (iv) Mohini clapped with joy when she saw the balloon.

   (v) Mohini was not able to draw a moon.

2. Tick (✓) the correct option.

   (i) Mohini was sitting with her grandmother one __________.

     (a) night   (b) morning

     (c) evening   (d) day

   (ii) The second thing drawn by the grandmother was a __________.

     (a) ball   (b) balloon

     (c) circle   (d) rabbit

(iii) Grandmother added a __________ line to the circle.

   (a) straight   (b) small

   (c) zig-zag   (d) long

(iv) Mohini also drew her own __________.

   (a) pet   (b) face

   (c) lace   (d) shoes

3. On the basis of the chapter, give answers to the following questions.

(i) What did grandmother and Mohini draw first? (Ball/Circle)

(ii) Who clapped with joy? (Grandmother/Mohini)

(iii) Does Mohini draw a wheel? (Yes/No)

Language Based Questions

4. Match the words in Column A with their opposites in Column B.

Column A	Column B
(i) Man	(a) Night
(ii) Grandmother	(b) Woman
(iii) Girl	(c) Sit
(iv) Stand	(d) Grandfather
(v) Day	(e) Boy

5. Look at the pictures. Rearrange the jumbled words to form meaningful words.

(i) LBAL   _______________ 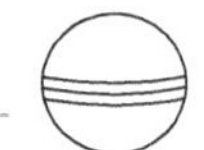

(ii) LLOOBNA   _______________ 

(iii) NSU   _______________ 

6. Write down the names of the shapes of the following things

(i) 

Earth

    C _ R _ L _

(ii) 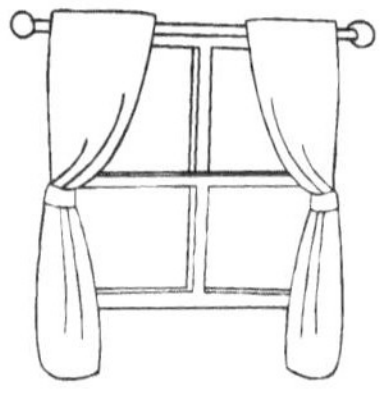

Window

    S _ U _ R _

(iii) 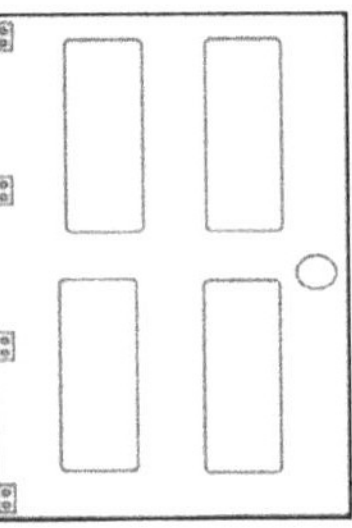

Door

    R _ C _ A _ G _ E

(iv) 

Cap

    T _ I _ N _ L _

01

If I Were an Apple

Text Based Questions

1. State 'T' for True and 'F' for False statement.

(i) The child wants to be an apple.

(ii) The apple does not want to drop down.

(iii) An apple grows on a mango tree.

(iv) The child wants to give joy to everyone.

(v) The apple would fall down on a bad boy.

2. Tick (✓) the correct option.

(i) Apples grow on ___________.

(a) an apple   (b) a plant

(c) a tree   (d) a cat

(ii) Why would the apple not stay on the tree?

    (a) As it does not like the tree

    (b) As it likes falling down

    (c) As it would give nobody joy

    (d) As it likes the nice boy

(iii) What would the child say if he was an apple?

    (a) Eat me, my boy!   (b) Eat me, my girl!

    (c) Don't eat me!   (d) Don't touch me!

3. On the basis of the poem, give answers to the following questions.

  (i) Do you like apples? (Yes/No)

____

  (ii) On whom does the apple want to fall down? (Girl/Boy)

____

4. Rearrange the jumbled words to form meaningful words.

  (i) WNOD   _________________________

  (ii) LEAPP   _________________________

  (iii) ICEN   _________________________

  (iv) EERT   _________________________

Language Based Questions

5. Circle the words which are spelled correctly.

    (i) Fall   Fele   Fol

    (ii) Apal   Apple   Appell

6. Match the words in Column A with their opposites in Column B.

	Column A		Column B
(i)	Nice	(a)	Sorrow
(ii)	Down	(b)	Girl
(iii)	Boy	(c)	Up
(iv)	Joy	(d)	Nasty

7. Fill in the blanks with the correct vowel from the box.

> a   e   i   o   u

    (i) Dr __ w   gr __ w   thr __ w

    (ii) b __ ll   f __ ll   c __ ll

    (iii) m __ w   f __ w   d __ w

8. Find the odd one out.

    (i) Mango, Grapes, Brinjal, Apple

    (ii) Cow, Cat, Donkey, Sparrow

    (iii) Eagle, Elephant, Parrot, Duck

    (iv) Mouth, Hand, Eyes, Body

02

Our Tree

Text Based Questions

1. State 'T' for True and 'F' for False statement.

   (i) The fruit on the tree was not ripe.

   (ii) The bird eats a tasty mango.

   (iii) A little plant was born from the seed.

   (iv) There were spider webs on the tree.

   (v) The tree had weak branches.

2. Tick (✓) the correct option.

   (i) The bird in the story is ____________.

     (a) big   (b) little

     (c) sad   (d) mad

   (ii) When the rains came, the children ____________.

     (a) ran   (b) clapped

     (c) danced   (d) played

(iii) The tree had long ________________.

    (a) leaves   (b) trunk

    (c) roots   (d) branches

(iv) The caterpillars had ________________ legs.

    (a) long   (b) tiny

    (c) strong   (d) ripe

(v) What did the children want to do with the fruit?

    (a) They wanted to see them fall

    (b) They wanted to play with them

    (c) They wanted to pluck them

    (d) They wanted the birds to eat them

3. On the basis of the poem, give answers to the following questions.

(i) Where was the ripe fruit? (Tree/Bird)

(ii) What kind of fruits did the tree have? (Sour/Ripe)

(iii) What does the little bird eat? (Berry/Ant)

(iv) What type of plant was born? (Big/Little)

(v) What did the crows do on the tree? (Perch/Run)

(vi) Who had fun on the tree? (Squirrels/Monkeys)

Language Based Questions

4. Match the words in Column A with their opposites in Column B.

	Column A		Column B
(i)	Ripe	(a)	Ugly
(ii)	Tall	(b)	Unripe
(iii)	Tiny	(c)	Short
(iv)	Rich	(d)	Huge
(v)	Strong	(e)	Poor
(vi)	Beautiful	(f)	Weak

5. Fill in the blanks.

(i) On a sunny day, we can see the __ U __.

(ii) On a clear night, we can see the M __ __ N and the S __ A __ S.

(iii) On a cloudy day, we can see the C __ O __ D __.

(iv) When it rains, we use an U __ B __ E __ L A.

(v) When it is very cold, we wear a S __ E __ T __ R.

01

A Kite

Text Based Questions

1. State 'T' for True and 'F' for False statement.

(i) The child wished to be the breeze.

(ii) The child often wished that he could be a kite in the sky.

(iii) The child did not like to ride on a breeze.

(iv) In the poem the child is flying a kite.

(v) The poem is about flying kites.

2. Tick (✓) the correct option.

(i) The child would often __________ and wish.

(a) stand   (b) play

(c) eat   (d) sit

(ii) The child wanted to be a kite up in the __________.

(a) playground   (b) school

(c) sky   (d) house

(iii) A kite rides upon the _________.

    (a) roof   (b) breeze

    (c) bird   (d) cat

3. On the basis of the poem, give answers to the following questions.

    (i) Where do kites fly? (Sky/Ground)

    (ii) What does the child wish to be? (Breeze/Kite)

Language Based Questions

4. Match the words in Column A with their plurals in Column B.

Column A	Column B
(i) Kite	(a) Cars
(ii) Child	(b) Kites
(iii) Dog	(c) Children
(iv) Car	(d) Leaves
(v) Leaf	(e) Dogs

5. Pick and write the things from the box which can fly.

pencil, kite, stone, rat, bird, chair, aeroplane, cat, fox, parrot, dog, shoes

The things which can fly are

    (i) _____________   (ii) _____________

    (iii) _____________   (iv) _____________

02

Sundari

Text Based Questions

1. State 'T' for True and 'F' for False statement.

   (i) Sundari was a big red, white and yellow kite.

   (ii) Bobby took Sundari to the fair one day.

   (iii) A merry-go-round was playing a sad little tune.

   (iv) Bobby looked for an open space.

2. Tick (✓) the correct option.

   (i) When Bobby made Sundari, she __________ at him.

     (a) laughed   (b) cried

     (c) looked   (d) smiled

   (ii) Bobby named his kite Sundari because she was __________ .

     (a) ugly   (b) fat

     (c) beautiful   (d) thin

   (iii) Bobby __________ the dog away.

     (a) shooed   (b) kicked

     (c) threw   (d) took

3. On the basis of the chapter, give answers to the following questions.

(i) What was the merry-go-round carrying? (Animals/Boys and Girls)

(ii) Who started to fly up? (Sundari/Bobby)

Language Based Questions

4. Fill in the blanks with the correct word from the box.

> band   Sundari   tugged   up

(i) The ________________ was playing at the fair.

(ii) ________________ leaped up in the air.

(iii) Sundari ________________ hard at her string.

(iv) Sundari flew ________________ in the air.

5. Match the words in Column A with their opposites in Column B.

Column A	Column B
(i) Smile	(a) Down
(ii) Open	(b) Frown
(iii) High	(c) Close
(iv) Happy	(d) Low
(v) Up	(e) Sad

01

A Little Turtle

Text Based Questions

1. State 'T' for True and 'F' for False statement.

   (i) The turtle is big.

   (ii) The turtle crawls very slowly.

   (iii) A turtle never gets tired.

2. Tick (✓) the correct option.

   (i) The poem is about a ___________ .

     (a) pig   (b) dog

     (c) rat   (d) turtle

   (ii) A turtle puts in his ___________ .

     (a) head   (b) legs

     (c) tail   (d) head, legs and tail

(iii) A turtle goes to bed when it is __________ .

    (a) tired   ☐   (b) night time   ☐

    (c) angry   ☐   (d) shy   ☐

3. On the basis of the poem, give answers for the following questions.

    (i) What does a turtle carry? (House/Bed)

    (ii) How does a turtle crawl? (Slow/Fast)

Language Based Questions

4. Look at the pictures and complete the sentences.

    (i) A Lion lives in a D __ __ .

    (ii) A Hen lives in a C__ __ P.

    (iii) A Horse lives in a __ T __ B __ E.

    (iv) A Cow lives in a S__ __ D.

02

The Tiger and the Mosquito

Text Based Questions

1. State 'T' for True and 'F' for False statement.

(i) A tiger was dozing in a cave.

(ii) The mosquito was afraid of the tiger.

(iii) The tiger was angry.

(iv) The tiger was not helpless.

(v) The mosquito told the tiger not to be so proud.

2. Tick (✓) the correct option.

(i) A mosquito came __________ by.

(a) mugging

(b) dancing

(c) playing

(d) buzzing

(ii) The tiger hit out with his _________.

    (a) jaw   (b) head

    (c) paw   (d) claw

(iii) The paw struck the tiger's own _________.

    (a) jaw   (b) cheek

    (c) chin   (d) head

(iv) Everyone is _________ in his own way.

    (a) great   (b) lazy

    (c) late   (d) big

3. Answer the following questions.

(i) Who was dozing under a tree? (Mosquito/Tiger)

____

(ii) What did the tiger do when he was angry? (Hit out/Go away)

____

(iii) What struck his own cheek? (Hand/Paw)

____

(iv) What did the mosquito continue to do? (Buzz/Walk away)

____

(v) Who flew off? (Tiger/Mosquito)

____

Language Based Questions

4. Match the words in Column A with their opposites in Column B.

Column A	Column B
(i) Under	(a) Brave
(ii) Angry	(b) Above
(iii) Great	(c) Calm
(iv) Friend	(d) Little
(v) Afraid	(e) Enemy

5. Match the animals in column A with their sounds in column B.

Column A	Column B
(i)	(a) Bleat-bleat
(ii)	(b) Roar-roar
(iii)	(c) Chirp-chirp
(iv)	(d) Buzz-buzz
(v)	(e) Chatter-chatter

01
Clouds

Text Based Questions

1. State 'T' for True and 'F' for False statement.

   (i) It was hot before it rained.

  (ii) The sky is orange.

 (iii) Clouds bring storm.

 (iv) The children sang and danced when it rained.

2. Tick (✓) the correct option.

  (i) A little cloud comes _____________ for you.

    (a) hooking   (b) cooking

    (c) hearing   (d) looking

 (ii) _____________ clouds come.

    (a) Store   (b) Few

    (c) More   (d) Four

(iii) Who brings rain?

    (a) Children   (b) Kittens

    (c) A boy   (d) Clouds

3. On the basis of the poem, give answers to the following questions.

(i) What do the clouds bring? (Rain/Storm)

(ii) What is the colour of the sky? (Yellow/Blue)

Language Based Questions

4. Fill in the blanks to complete the words taken from the poem.

(i) H __ T

(ii) S __ Y

(iii) C __ O U D

(iv) R __ I N

(v) C __ O L

(vi) B R __ __ G

(vii) D __ __ C E

(viii) S __ __ G

5. Write the colours of the following.

(i) Sky

(ii) Water

(iii) Soil

02 Anandi's Rainbow

Text Based Questions

1. State 'T' for True and 'F' for False statement.

   (i) It was not raining outside.

   (ii) Anandi was fast asleep.

   (iii) There was a dull rainbow outside.

   (iv) Anandi loved to draw and paint.

   (v) The rainbow was gone after giving colours to the flowers and the Sun.

2. Tick (✓) the correct option.

   (i) Anandi woke up to look out of her ______________.

     (a) door   (b) window

     (c) room   (d) balcony

   (ii) Anandi ran out to the garden with ______________.

     (a) Milli   (b) Billi

     (c) Silly   (d) her mother

(iii) Anandi wanted to paint the flowers of her garden with the colours of the __________ .

    (a) sky   (b) wall

    (c) her dress   (d) rainbow

(iv) Anandi left the _______ colour.

    (a) violet   (b) indigo

    (c) yellow   (d) red

(v) The _______ was shining in its yellow glory.

    (a) Sun   (b) Moon

    (c) Earth   (d) Stars

3. On the basis of the chapter, give answers to the following questions.

(i) What was Anandi dreaming of? (Rainbows/Colours)

(ii) Who was Milli? (Dog/Cat)

(iii) Where did Anandi run out? (House/Garden)

(iv) Which colour did Anandi use to paint the leaves? (Green/Blue)

(v) What kind of flowers were there all over the garden? (Beautiful/Ugly)

Language Based Questions

4. Circle the correctly spelled words from the following.

	A	B	C
(i)	Autsid	Outside	Outsyde
(ii)	Dream	Dreem	Dreame
(iii)	Rainboo	Rainbow	Rainbovw
(iv)	Brite	Brightt	Bright
(v)	Clear	Klear	Clearr

5. Circle the odd one out.

(i) Cat, Bat, Mat, Sun, Fat

(ii) Red, Green, Fox, Yellow, Orange

(iii) Sun, Moon, Stars, Clouds, House

(iv) Flower, Fruit, Leaves, Ball, Branches

(v) Clear, Fear, Boat, Near, Dear

6. Complete the words by filling the missing letters.

(i) S __ Y

(ii) O __ T

(iii) F __ ST

(iv) B __ IGHT

(v) F __ OW __ R

(vi) DR __ W

7. Look at the picture and answer the questions that follow. Also, colour the picture.

   (i) Name the girl and the cat in the picture.

   (ii) What is the girl doing?

01

Flying-Man

Text Based Questions

1. State 'T' for True and 'F' for False statement.

(i) The Flying-man flies over the sea.

(ii) The child does not speak with the Flying-man.

(iii) The Flying-man wants to fly over the building.

(iv) The child wants to go with the Flying-man.

(v) The Flying-man never flies.

2. Tick (✓) the correct option.

(i) The Flying-man is _______ in the sky.

(a) down   (b) up

(c) upto   (d) over

(ii) The Flying-man flies _____________.

(a) low   (b) out

(c) high   (d) under

(iii) The Flying-man flies over ________________ .

    (a) building   ☐   (b) mountains   ☐

    (c) sea   ☐   (d) mountains and sea   ☐

3. On the basis of the chapter, give answers to the following questions.

  (i) What does the child ask the Flying-man?

  (ii) What does the child wish for?

Language Based Questions

4. Match the words in Column A with their opposites in Column B.

Column A	Column B
(i) Man	(a) Can
(ii) Up	(b) Woman
(iii) High	(c) Down
(iv) Can't	(d) Low

5. Think and write a few words that end with 'man'. The first one has been done for you.

(i) Postman   (ii) ____________   (iii) ____________

(iv) ____________   (v) ____________

6. Look at the pictures and write their names.

(i) M__U__T__I__   (ii) H__U__E

02

The Tailor and his Friend

Text Based Questions

1. State 'T' for True and 'F' for False statement.

(i) Kalu's shop was near the school.

(ii) Kalu was a tailor.

(iii) Appu came to Kalu's shop everyday.

(iv) Kalu did not play any trick on Appu.

(v) Appu threw garbage in Kalu's shop.

2. Tick (✓) the correct option.

(i) Kalu made clothes for _______________.

(a) men   (b) women

(c) children   (d) Appu

(ii) Kalu pricked Appu's _________________.

    (a) tail   ☐   (b) ears   ☐

    (c) head   ☐   (d) trunk   ☐

(iii) An elephant never _________________.

    (a) forgets   ☐   (b) cheats   ☐

    (c) sleeps   ☐   (d) sits   ☐

(iv) Appu came to Kalu's shop after _________ days.

    (a) one   ☐   (b) two   ☐

    (c) three   ☐   (d) four   ☐

(v) All the new clothes became _________________.

    (a) wet   ☐   (b) dry   ☐

    (c) set   ☐   (d) dirty   ☐

3. On the basis of the chapter give answers to the following questions.

    (i) What type of pants did Kalu make? (Dirty/Colourful)

    (ii) What did Kalu give Appu to eat? (Nice Things/Bad things)

    (iii) Who was Appu? (Tailor/Elephant)

    (iv) Who became good friends? (Kalu and Appu/Tailor and Kalu)

    (v) Who ran away in pain? (Appu/Kalu)

Language Based Questions

4. Count and identify the things/people/animals shown in the pictures below and write them. The first one has been done for you.

(i) Three trees   (ii) ________________

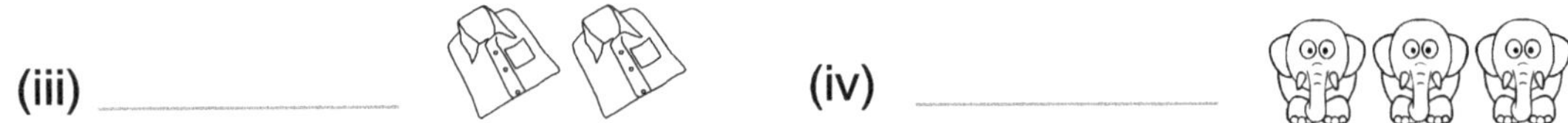

(iii) ________________   (iv) ________________

5. Look at the picture and answer the questions that follow. Also, colour the picture.

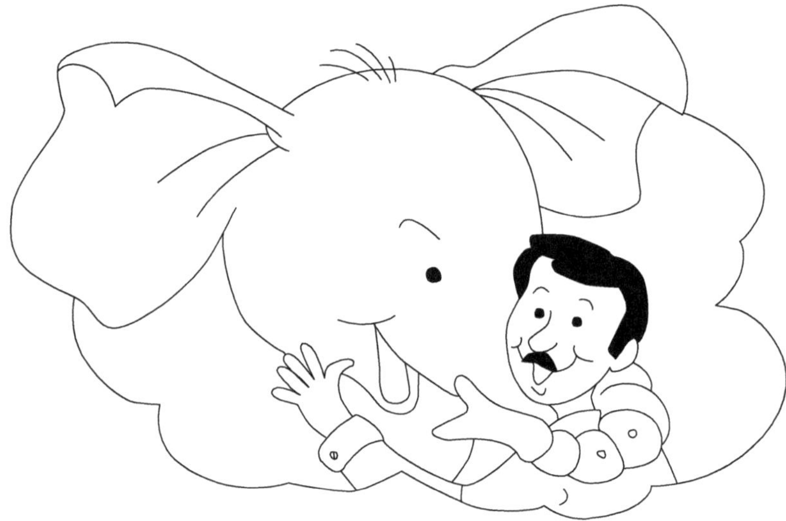

(i) Who are there in the picture?

____

(ii) What are they doing?

____

01

Vowels and Consonants

The letters a, e, i, o, u are called Vowels.

When sounding vowels, your breath flows freely through your mouth.

The rest of the letters b, c, d, f, g, h, j, k, l, m, n, p, q, r, s, t, v, w, x, y, z are called as Consonants.

Some of the words which have vowels in them are

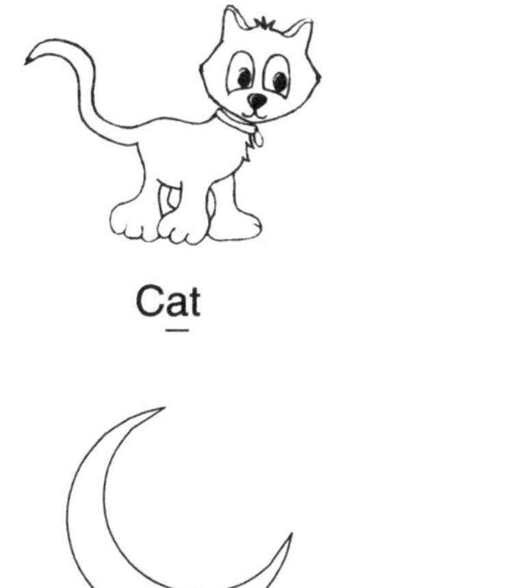

Cat

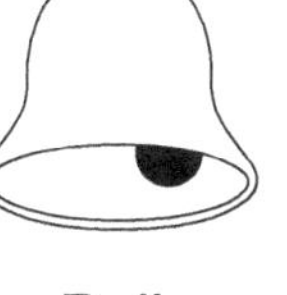

Bell

Fish

Moon

Sun

1. Complete the names of the pictures by filling in the missing vowels.

(i) __ gg 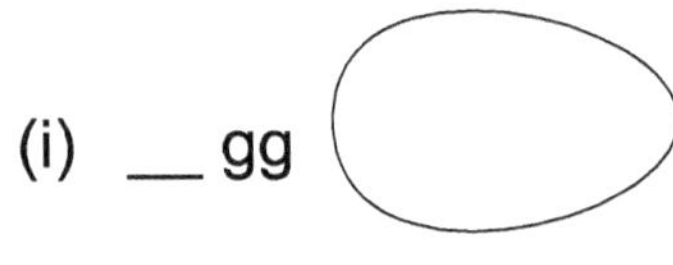

(ii) C __ p 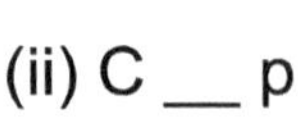

(iii) D __ ll 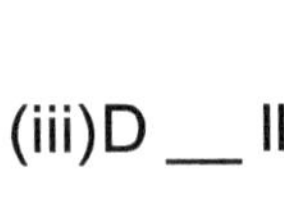

(iv) K __ ng 

(v) G __ t __ 

(vi) G __ __ t 

(vii) P __ n 

(viii) K __ y 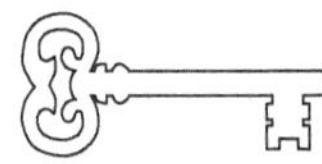

(ix) W __ ll 

(x) Sp __ __ n 

(xi) C __ p 

(xii) B __ __ t 

2. Fill in the blanks with correct vowel from the box.

a   e   i   o   u

(i) h __ n   p __ n   t __ n   d __ n

(ii) c __ t   b __ t   r __ t   s __ t

02

Articles

The words 'A', 'An' and 'The' are called Articles.

'A' is used before words beginning with a consonant.

Examples

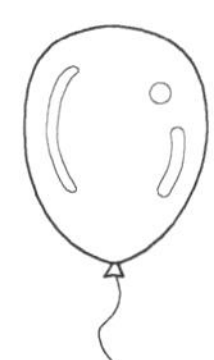

A Fish   A Flower   A Balloon   A Cat

'An' is used before words beginning with a vowel.

Examples

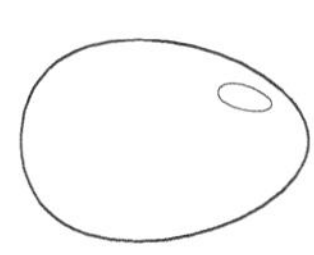

An Egg   An Apple   An Umbrella   An Igloo

'The' is used before words such as

The Sun

The Moon

The Stars

The Earth

Articles (A, An, The)

1. Put a tick (✓) if 'a' or 'an' is correctly used or a (✗) if not.

(i) ☐ An orange   (ii) ☐ A flower

(iii) ☐ A umbrella   (iv) ☐ An eggs

(v) ☐ A photo   (vi) ☐ An actor

(vii) ☐ An aeroplane   (viii) ☐ A cap

(ix) ☐ A ice-cream   (x) ☐ A jacket

(xi) ☐ An owl   (xii) ☐ A balls

(xiii) ☐ A bottle   (xiv) ☐ An inkpot

(xv) ☐ An apples   (xvi) ☐ A biscuits

(xvii) ☐ A joker   (xviii) ☐ A tailor

(xix) ☐ A cats   (xx) ☐ A turtle

(xxi) ☐ A shops   (xxii) ☐ An eye

(xxiii) ☐ A toffees   (xxiv) ☐ A teacher

(xxv) ☐ A boys   (xxvi) ☐ A girl

2. Do you use 'a' or 'an' before these words?
Write your answers in the given spaces.

(i) _______ table   (ii) _______ inkpot

(iii) _______ telephone   (iv) _______ envelope

(v) _______ train   (vi) _______ pencil

(vii) _______ insect   (viii) _______ mask

03

Nouns
(Naming-Words)

The words which are used as names of persons, animals, places or things are called nouns.

All naming-words are nouns. Some examples of nouns are

Names of people Amit, Payal, Ravi

Names of animals Cow, Dog, Cat

Names of places Delhi, Home, School

Names of things Tea, Chalk, Bread

Exercise

1. Separate the nouns given in the box into four lists.

    (i) Persons   (ii) Animals   (iii) Places   (iv) Things

> Mat, Fox, Raj, India, House, Rashmi, Table, Monkey, Hospital, Cake, Socks, Tiger, School, Rabbit, Nisha, Shalini

2. Circle the odd one out from the words mentioned in the clouds.

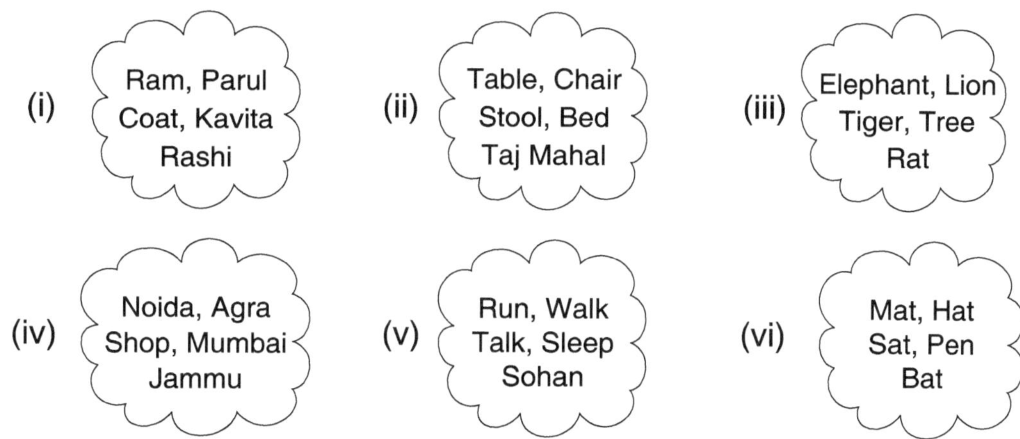

3. Find the nouns from the words given in the box.

> Eat, Soap, Good, Sonam, Owl, Play, Old, Jaipur, Pretty, Chocolate, Walk, Baby, She, Toothpaste

The nouns in the box are

04 Pronouns

Pronouns are words that are used instead of Nouns.

We use pronouns so that we do not have to use the names everytime we address a person. Examples of pronouns are: I, Me, You, His, Her, He, She, Him, They, Them, Their, Our, It, etc.

Exercise

1. Find the pronouns from the words given in the box.

> Rohan, I, His, Sad, Come, Green, Her, Peelu, Coat, Him, Take,
> Shake, They, My, Can, Climb, Monkey, Lizard, Your, Me

The pronouns in the box are

(i) _____________________   (ii) _____________________

(iii) _____________________   (iv) _____________________

(v) _____________________   (vi) _____________________

(vii) _____________________   (viii) _____________________

2. Underline the pronouns in the sentences given below.

(i) 

Ravi decided to paint them yellow.

(ii) 

The man gave the kitty to her.

(iii) 

The doctor asked him to take a deep breath.

(iv) 

The class liked our song and clapped for us.

(v) 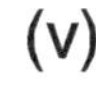

Manish pulled it out from the hat.

(vi) 

Bob looked at it.

3. Replace the underlined words with He, She or It.

    (i) The boy played games after dinner.

    ________ played games after dinner.

    (ii) The cat climbed onto the kitchen table.

    ________ climbed onto the kitchen table.

    (iii) My brother is in high school.

    ________ is in high school.

4. Fill in the blanks using Has or Have.

    (i) I _______________ two brothers.

    (ii) He _______________ a pencil.

    (iii) Do you _______________ a raincoat?

    (iv) They _______________ a big house.

    (v) She _______________ got my bag.

05

Doing-Words
(Verbs)

The words which show an action are called as Doing-Words or Verbs.
Examples of doing-words are play, study, walk, talk, sleep, run, etc.

The pictures below show some Doing-Words (Verbs).

Read

Write

Cook

Play

Cry

Sleep

Exercise

1. Find the verbs from the list of words given in the box.

> Sweet, Run, Amit, Talk, Played, Lovely, Eat, Pray
> John, Mohini, Draw, Laugh, Smile, Aditya, Sonam, Delhi

The verbs in the box are

(i) ________________________   (ii) ________________________

(iii) ________________________   (iv) ________________________

(v) ________________________   (vi) ________________________

(vii) ________________________   (viii) ________________________

2. Write the doing-words by looking at the pictures given below. The first one has been done for you.

(i) Exercise   (ii) R__d__   (iii) B__u__h   (iv) J__m__

(v) S__a__d   (vi) K__c__   (vii) F__y   (viii) R__n

06

Describing-Words
(Adjectives)

The words which describe something are called Describing-Words or Adjectives.

e.g. big, small, tall, short, young, old, good, bad, beautiful, ugly, etc

Look at the pictures given below.

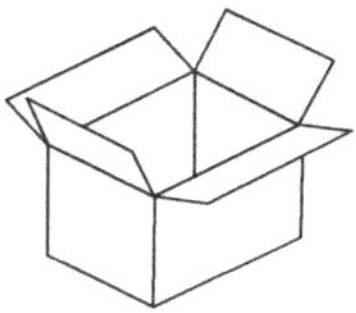

An Open Box

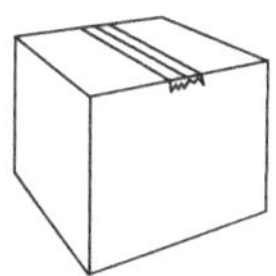

A Closed Box

A Happy Face

A Sad Face

A Fast Bus

A Slow Snail

A Big Tree

A Cold Ice Cube

Exercise

1. Find the adjectives from the words listed in the box.

> Cup, Small, Dig, Bat, School, Big, Pretty, Her, Office,
> Garden, Bad, Rich, Shop, Him, She, Happy

The adjectives in the box are

(i) _______________________   (ii) _______________________

(iii) _______________________   (iv) _______________________

(v) _______________________   (vi) _______________________

2. Write the adjectives below into the correct column.

> Hard, Sad, Angry, Tiny, Rough, Purple, Spicy, Scared, Lonely, Round,
> Confused, Sour, Excited, Sweet, Bitter, Oily, Large, Salty

Things	Feelings	Tastes

3. Underline the adjective in each sentence.

(i) The boy played with his green kite.

(ii) The wet dog was playing in the water.

(iii) We saw the funny clown play guitar.

(iv) The red apple had a worm inside.

(v) It was a clean pond for the animals.

07
Prepositions

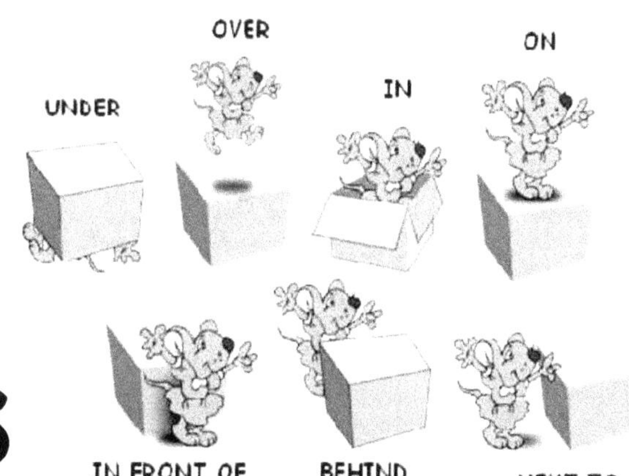

The words which show the relation of one thing to another are called Prepositions.

e.g. in, on, over, under, behind, in front of, between, near, below, above, etc.

Exercise

1. Choose the prepositions from the words given in the box.

> Sohini, On, And, Pretty, Walking, If, Above, But,
> Sleep, Monu, As, Under, House, Ugly, In, Ball

The prepositions in the box are

(i) _____________   (ii) _____________

(iii) _____________   (iv) _____________

2. Choose the correct prepositions from the brackets to complete the sentences.

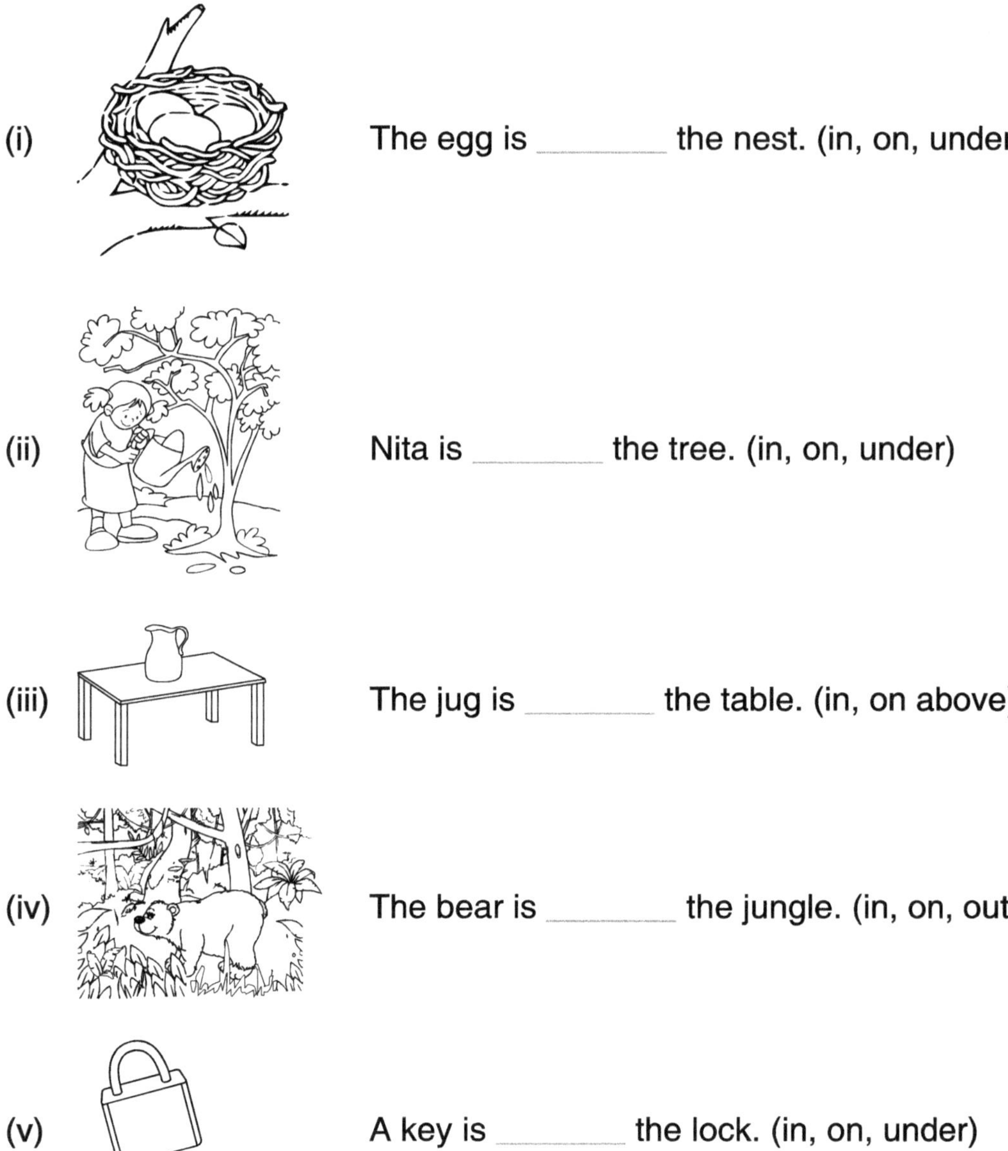

(i) The egg is _________ the nest. (in, on, under)

(ii) Nita is _________ the tree. (in, on, under)

(iii) The jug is _________ the table. (in, on above)

(iv) The bear is _________ the jungle. (in, on, out)

(v) A key is _________ the lock. (in, on, under)

Answer Sheet

(Section A)

Unit 1

Chapter 1 A Happy Child

1. (i) T   (ii) F   (iii) F   (iv) F   (v) T
2. (i) (d)   (ii) (c)   (iii) (b)   (iv) (a)
3. (i) Sits   (ii) Green
4. (i) B   (ii) A   (iii) C   (iv) A   (v) B   (vi) C
5. (i) Tree   (ii) House (iii) Sun
6. (i) RED   (ii) PLAY   (iii) DAY   (iv) LAUGH (v) GREEN   (vi) SUN
7. (i) Door   (ii) Windows (iii) Roof

Chapter 2 Three Little Pigs

1. (i) F   (ii) T   (iii) F   (iv) T   (v) F
2. (i) (d)   (ii) (c)   (iii) (b)   (iv) (a)
3. (i) Sticks (ii) Wolf   (iii) Sonu and Monu   (iv) Sonu, Monu and Gonu
   (v) Red
4. (i) (d)   (ii) (c)   (iii) (e)   (iv) (a)   (v) (b)
5. (i) B   (ii) A   (iii) B   (iv) C   (v) C   (vi) A

Unit 2

Chapter 1 After A Bath

1. (i) F   (ii) T   (iii) F   (iv) T
2. (i) wipe   (ii) toes   (iii) two   (iv) shiny
3. (i) (b)   (ii) (d)   (iii) (c)
4. (i) Two   (ii) Yes   (iii) Hands
5. (i) B   (ii) C   (iii) C   (iv) A   (v) B   (vi) C
6. (i) Wet   (ii) Dull   (iii) More   (iv) Before
7. (i) BUCKET (ii) TOWEL (iii) SOAP

Chapter 2 The Bubble, the Straw and the Shoe

1. (i) F   (ii) F   (iii) T   (iv) T   (v) F
2. (i) (b)   (ii) (c)   (iii) (d)
3. (i) Forest (ii) Shoe   (iii) Straw

4. (i) C   (ii) B   (iii) A   (iv) B

5. (i) (b)   (ii) (c)   (iii) (d)   (iv) (e)   (v) (a)

6. (i) TIME   (ii) SHOE   (iii) RIVER   (iv) FLOAT   (v) YOU   (vi) CROSS

Unit 3

Chapter 1 One Little Kitten

1. (i) F   (ii) T   (iii) F   (iv) T   (v) F

2. (i) (b)   (ii) (d)   (iii) (a)   (iv) (a)

3. (i) Nine   (ii) Big   (iii) Baby

4. (i) B   (ii) C   (iii) A   (iv) B   (v) A

5. (i) Butterflies (ii) Kittens   (iii) Fishes or Fish   (iv) Rats   (v) Seagulls

6. (i) (b)   (ii) (c)   (iii) (a)   (iv) (e)   (v) (d)

7. (i) ONE   (ii) BABY   (iii) FOUR   (iv) SAD   (v) SILLY   (vi) BEES
   (vii) TAILS

Chapter 2 Lalu and Peelu

1. (i) T   (ii) F   (iii) T   (iv) F   (v) T   (vi) F

2. (i) (b)   (ii) (c)   (iii) (d)   (iv) (c)

3. (i) Yellow   (ii) Red Chilli   (iii) Screamed (iv) Red

4. (i) Chicks   (ii) Thing   (iii) Plant   (iv) Scream   (v) Gobble   (vi) Brought

5. (i) (d)   (ii) (c)   (iii) (b)   (iv) (a)

Unit 4

Chapter 1 Once I Saw a Little Bird

1. (i) F   (ii) T   (iii) T   (iv) F   (v) F

2. (i) (d)   (ii) (c)   (iii) (a)   (iv) (c)

3. (i) Little bird   (ii) Shook

4. (i) Large or Big (ii) Stop   (iii) Come   (iv) Laugh

Chapter 2 Mittu and the Yellow Mango

1. (i) F   (ii) T   (iii) F   (iv) T   (v) F

2. (i) (d)   (ii) (c)   (iii) (b)   (iv) (a)

3. (i) Mangoes   (ii) On tree   (iii) Crow   (iv) Balloon

4. (i) B   (ii) A   (iii) B   (iv) C   (v) C   (vi) B
   (vii) C   (viii) C

5. (i) (b)   (ii) (e)   (iii) (d)   (iv) (c)   (v) (a)

Unit 5

Chapter 1 Merry-Go-Round

1. (i) F   (ii) T   (iii) F   (iv) T
2. (i) (b)   (ii) (c)
3. (i) Horse   (ii) Round and round
4. (i) B   (ii) C   (iii) B   (iv) A   (v) C
5. (i) Small   (ii) Stand   (iii) Under   (iv) Black

Chapter 2 Circle

1. (i) T   (ii) F   (iii) F   (iv) T   (v) F
2. (i) (d)   (ii) (a)   (iii) (c)   (iv) (b)
3. (i) Circle   (ii) Mohini   (iii) Yes
4. (i) (b)   (ii) (d)   (iii) (e)   (iv) (c)   (v) (a)
5. (i) BALL   (ii) BALLOON (iii) SUN
6. (i) CIRCLE   (ii) SQUARE   (iii) RECTANGLE   (iv) TRIANGLE

Unit 6

Chapter 1 If I Were an Apple

1. (i) T   (ii) F   (iii) F   (iv) T   (v) F
2. (i) (c)   (ii) (c)   (iii) (a)
3. (i) Yes (Your answer can be different)   (ii) Boy
4. (i) Down   (ii) Apple   (iii) Nice   (iv) Tree
5. (i) Fall   (ii) Apple
6. (i) (d)   (ii) (c)   (iii) (b)   (iv) (a)
7. (i) drew, grew, threw   (ii) ball, fall, call   (iii) mew, few, dew
8. (i) Brinjal (ii) Sparrow (iii) Elephant (iv) Body

Chapter 2 Our Tree

1. (i) F   (ii) F   (iii) T   (iv) T   (v) F
2. (i) (b)   (ii) (a)   (iii) (d)   (iv) (b)   (v) (c)
3. (i) Tree   (ii) Ripe   (iii) Berry   (iv) Little   (v) Perch   (vi) Monkeys
4. (i) (b)   (ii) (c)   (iii) (d)   (iv) (e)   (v) (f)   (vi) (a)
5. (i) SUN   (ii) MOON, STARS   (iii) CLOUDS   (iv) UMBRELLA
    (v) SWEATER

Unit 7

Chapter 1 A Kite

1. (i) F (ii) T (iii) F (iv) F (v) F
2. (i) (d) (ii) (c) (iii) (b) 3. (i) Sky (ii) Kite
4. (i) (b) (ii) (c) (iii) (e) (iv) (a) (v) (d)
5. (i) Kite (ii) Bird (iii) Aeroplane (iv) Parrot

Chapter 2 Sundari

1. (i) F (ii) T (iii) F (iv) T
2. (i) (d) (ii) (c) (iii) (a)
3. (i) Boys and Girls (ii) Sundari
4. (i) band (ii) Sundari (iii) tugged (iv) up
5. (i) (b) (ii) (c) (iii) (d) (iv) (e) (v) (a)

Unit 8

Chapter 1 A Little Turtle

1. (i) F (ii) T (iii) F
2. (i) (d) (ii) (d) (iii) (a)
3. (i) House (ii) Slow
4. (i) DEN (ii) COOP (iii) STABLE (iv) SHED

Chapter 2 The Tiger and the Mosquito

1. (i) F (ii) F (iii) T (iv) F (v) T
2. (i) (d) (ii) (c) (iii) (b) (iv) (a)
3. (i) Tiger (ii) Hit out (iii) Paw (iv) Buzz (v) Mosquito
4. (i) (b) (ii) (c) (iii) (d) (iv) (e) (v) (a)
5. (i) (b) (ii) (e) (iii) (d) (iv) (a) (v) (c)

Unit 9

Chapter 1 Clouds

1. (i) T (ii) F (iii) F (iv) T
2. (i) (d) (ii) (c) (iii) (d) 3. (i) Rain (ii) Blue
4. (i) HOT (ii) SKY (iii) CLOUD (iv) RAIN (v) COOL (vi) BRING (vii) DANCE (viii) SING
5. (i) Blue (ii) Colourless (iii) Brown

Chapter 2 Anandi's Rainbow

1.	(i) F	(ii) T	(iii) F	(iv) T	(v) T
2.	(i) (b)	(ii) (a)	(iii) (d)	(iv) (c)	(v) (a)
3.	(i) Rainbows	(ii) Cat	(iii) Garden	(iv) Green	(v) Beautiful
4.	(i) B	(ii) A	(iii) B	(iv) C	(v) A
5.	(i) Sun	(ii) Fox	(iii) House	(iv) Ball	(v) Boat

6. (i) SKY   (ii) OUT   (iii) FAST   (iv) BRIGHT   (v) FLOWER   (vi) DRAW

Unit 10

Chapter 1 Flying-Man

1.	(i) T	(ii) F	(iii) F	(iv) T	(v) F
2.	(i) (b)	(ii) (c)	(iii) (d)		
4.	(i) (b)	(ii) (c)	(iii) (d)	(iv) (a)	

5. (ii) Policeman   (iii) Fireman   (iv) Milkman   (v) Chairman

6. (i) MOUNTAIN (ii) HOUSE

Chapter 2 The Tailor and his Friend

1.	(i) F	(ii) T	(iii) T	(iv) F	(v) F
2.	(i) (c)	(ii) (d)	(iii) (a)	(iv) (b)	(v) (a)

3. (i) Colourful   (ii) Nice Things (iii) Elephant   (iv) Kalu and Appu   (v) Appu

4. (ii) Four needles   (iii) Two shirts   (iv) Three elephants

(Section B)

Chapter 1 Vowels

1. (i) Egg   (ii) Cup   (iii) Doll   (iv) King   (v) Gate   (vi) Goat
(vii) Pan   (viii) Key   (ix) Well   (x) Spoon   (xi) Cap   (xii) Boat

2. (i) hen, pen, ten, den   (ii) cat, bat, rat, sat

Chapter 2 Articles (A, An, The)

1. (i) (✓)   (ii) (✓)   (iii) (✗)   (iv) (✗)   (v) (✓)   (vi) (✓)
(vii) (✓)   (viii) (✓)   (ix) (✗)   (x) (✓)   (xi) (✓)   (xii) (✗)
(xiii) (✓)   (xiv) (✓)   (xv) (✗)   (xvi) (✗)   (xvii) (✓)   (xviii) (✓)
(xix) (✗)   (xx) (✓)   (xxi) (✗)   (xxii) (✓)   (xxiii) (✗)   (xxiv) (✓)
(xxv) (✗)   (xxvi) (✓)

2. (i) A   (ii) An   (iii) A   (iv) An   (v) A   (vi) A
(vii) An   (viii) A

Chapter 3 Nouns (Naming-Words)

1. Persons : Raj, Rashmi, Nisha, Shalini   Animals : Fox, Monkey, Tiger, Rabbit
   Places : India, House, Hospital, School   Things : Mat, Table, Cake, Socks
2. (i) Coat   (ii) Taj Mahal   (iii) Tree   (iv) Shop   (v) Sohan   (vi) Sat
3. Soap, Sonam, Owl, Jaipur, Chocolate, Baby, Toothpaste

Chapter 4 Pronouns

1. (i) I   (ii) His   (iii) Her   (iv) Him   (v) They   (vi) My
   (vii) Your   (viii) Me
2. (i) them   (ii) her   (iii) him   (iv) our, us   (v) it   (vi) it
3. (i) He   (ii) It   (iii) He
4. (i) have   (ii) has   (iii) have   (iv) have   (v) has

Chapter 5 Doing-Words (Verbs)

1. (i) Run   (ii) Talk   (iii) Played   (iv) Eat   (v) Pray   (vi) Draw
   (vii) Laugh (viii) Smile
2. (ii) Ride   (iii) Brush   (iv) Jump   (v) Stand   (vi) Kick   (vii) Fly
   (viii) Run

Chapter 6 Describing-Words (Adjectives)

1. (i) Small   (ii) Big   (iii) Pretty   (iv) Bad   (v) Rich   (vi) Happy
2. Things : Hard, Tiny, Rough, Purple, Round, Large
   Feelings : Sad, Angry, Scared, Lonely, Confused, Excited
   Tastes : Spicy, Sour, Sweet, Bitter, Oily, Salty
3. (i) green   (ii) wet   (iii) funny   (iv) red   (v) clean

Chapter 7 Prepositions

1. (i) On   (ii) Above   (iii) Under   (iv) In
2. (i) in   (ii) under   (iii) on   (iv) in   (v) in

www.ingramcontent.com/pod-product-compliance
Lightning Source LLC
LaVergne TN
LVHW080437200726
843507LV00004B/847